WITHDRAWN

W9-DIJ-145

Best wishes
Mary Calvert

Maine

captured
in color

Dedicated to my husband, Francis,
with love and appreciation for his
unlimited encouragement and support.

Mary R. Calvert

ISBN 0-9609914-1-7
Library of Congress No. 79-57050
Copyright 1980 by Mary R. Calvert
Revised edition copyright 1983

Printed by Twin City Printery
Lewiston, Maine

Mainstays of Maine

Maine is a bright place, and people have lived in it for a long time. And when people live in a place for a long time, they grow to be like it. The dishes they cook up grow to be like it, too. Maine is bayberry and sweetfern and fern-brake and balsams, and I like to think its people and their foods are pungent and sharp-flavored also. A Maine blueberry cannot help smelling like pitch-pines on a scorching hot day, for it ripened on just such a day and among those pines. . . .

Robert P. Tristram Coffin

Maine
captured
in color

moods and scenics . . .

Sixteen Going on Seventeen

Where, oh where does my fortune lie?
Shall I glimpse my future in a pearly
shell? Or in the glistening Sea?

Newagen Sunset

Hikers sit on the flat ledges below Big Niagara Falls enjoying the sight and sound of the falling water. This is part of a half mile stretch of the Nesowadnehunk River that drops 400 feet. There are two waterfalls with continuous cataracts between them.

Canoeing on Kidney Pond.

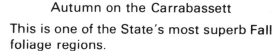
Autumn on the Carrabassett

This is one of the State's most superb Fall foliage regions.

The Carrabassett River is a delightful, rock strewed, birch lined, tributary of the Kennebec. It wends its way from the North slope of Sugarloaf Mountain through Kingfield, the New Portlands, under the historic Wire Bridge, and between fields and farmlands of pastoral beauty to enter its parent river at North Anson.

The Carrabassett's banks are literally lined with beautiful white birches and maples which provide a colorful spectacle in October.

Sundown on the Carrabassett provides us with a pool of burnished gold.

Ledges near Kingfield.

The Legend of Moosehead Lake

How beautiful the morning breaks
Upon the King of mountain lakes!
The forests, far as eye can reach,
Stretch green and still from either beach,
And leagues away the waters gleam
Resplendent in the sunrise beam!
Yet feathery vapors, circling slow,
Wreathe the dark brow of Kineo.

by Frances Laughton Mace

The Forest Floor

John Muir covered most of the American wilderness on foot,
without even a sleeping bag and for food only bread and tea.
He, of all our naturalists, loved and understood the forests best.
He was the most perceptive of travelers studying in minute detail the tracks
of small animals, including the tiny lizard which he said made the most beautiful
embroidery designs only ⅝ in. wide,
and which he had to lie down on the earth to see.

The most mundane things of the wild became beautiful when described by him.

"The mountain winds, like the dew and rain, sunshine and snow,
are measured and bestowed with love on the forests
to develop their strength and beauty.
— — —

The winds go to every tree, fingering every leaf and branch and furrowed bole;
not one is forgotten; the Mountain Pine towering with outstretched arms
on the rugged buttresses of the icy peaks,
the lowliest and most retiring tenant of the dells;
they seek and find them all, caressing them tenderly, — — —

the winds blessing the forests, the forests the winds,
with ineffable beauty and harmony as the sure result."

A soft white blanket of fog has dropped down over Back Cove
And the faint measured tone of the fog-horn sounds in the distance.

View of Mount Bigelow Range from Eustis Ridge.

Country Road

Where does the lure of a country road lie? Perhaps the spirit of adventure calls as many are unmarked and little traveled.

Who knows what sights may be around the next curve or over the next hilltop. A pond with waving grasses or pond lilies — a gurgling rocky little brook — falling over itself on its rush down the hillside.

The wood only whispers its song of waving fern and brake and leaves and the thin trill of a song bird.

The brook splashes and gurgles as it flows over the many stones and ledges. It breaks the cathedral like silence of the pine grove with only the soft rustling of its needles brushing against each other in the light breeze.

The trees on a real country road hug tightly to the edges and even sometimes form an arch overhead with the light which filters through the leaves dancing on the roadway with a play of sunlight and shadow, ever moving, ever changing.

On the Arnold Trail near Middle Carry Pond.

. . . But such a tide as moving seems asleep,
   Too full for sound and foam,
When that which drew from out the boundless deep
   Turns again home.

                            Alfred Lord Tennyson

A splash of Autumn-Kidney Pond looking toward Mount Katahdin

Summery reflections

Sandy Stream near Middle Carry Pond on the Arnold Trail.

To sit on rocks, to muse o'er flood and fell;
To slowly trace the forest's shady scene,
Where things that own not man's dominion dwell,
And mortal foot hath ne'er or rarely been!
To climb the trackless mountain all unseen,
With the wild flock, that never needs a fold;
Alone o'er steeps and foaming falls to lean;
This is not solitude; tis but to hold
Converse with Nature's charms, and view her stones unrolled.

Lord Byron

A Somerset County Back Road
Norridgewock to Starks

The drama of an approaching storm unfolds as the lone tree
bends furiously to and fro!

The waves build up and under the force
of the wind are driven into every nook
and cranny of the shore with a noise
like thunder!

"Ice Out" is the cry
that once rang out,
up and down the rivers,
to signal the start of
the log drives, now
a thing of the past.

The Carrabassett rises on the north slope
of Sugarloaf Mountain and winds through
farmlands and woods to enter the
Kennebec River at North Anson.

A woodland cabin — Eustis Ridge

Maine
**captured
in color**

the farmland . . .

Solitude
By Alexander Pope

Happy the man, whose wish and care
A few paternal acres bound,
Content to breathe his native air
In his own ground.

Whose herds with milk,
Whose fields with bread,
Whose flocks supply him with attire;
Whose trees in summer yield him shade,
In winter, fire.

Dependable horse power — Mayfield, Somerset County

Back to the "Good Old Days" splitting wood at Lakewood.

Lincoln County Barnyard, Dresden

Our early Maine farmers were practical and liked to avoid the discomfort of plowing through snowdrifts to do their chores on a cold winter morning, or to get wood to replenish the kitchen stove.

Thus the distinctive Maine connected farmhouses came into being. House, woodshed (which had other uses when the children acted up) and the cow barn were all under the same roof.

Maine
**captured
in color**

children . . .

Thank Heaven
for
Little Girls
and
Little Boys
too.

Playing beside a quiet pool.

Pulling up the dinghy in an East Boothbay cove.

Brownies on Parade. Memorial Day, Madison.

Do you remember the feel of soft, wet sand squishing between your toes?

The Captain navigates his craft through a narrow and dangerous channel.

In Stonington lobstermen's children play with — what else — but miniature self-made lobster boats.

Maine
captured
in color

up the kennebec . . .

An Arnold Expedition Re-enactment soldier looks out over Dead River from Cathedral Pines in Stratton.

The Arnold Expedition Re-enactment

The Bicentennial Year ushered in a great resurgence of patriotic feeling among Americans across the country.

The Arnold Expedition Historical Society of Maine planned and carried out one of the most elaborate of the Revolutionary War re-enactments.

Over 600 people took part, and in authentic costumes including replicas of powder loaded muskets, they followed the path of the original army for 10 days, ending with a mock battle on the Plains of Abraham in Quebec. There, as did the original army they lost the battle, but they did not, as did the soldiers of 1775, end up dead or in Quebec prisons.

The re-enactment army travelled up the Kennebec and Dead rivers in Maine and paraded in the following towns along the rivers: Bath, Augusta, Winslow, Waterville, Skowhegan, Norridgewock, Madison, Solon, Bingham, Kingfield, and Stratton. Bateau races and demonstrations were given in Madison, Cathedral Pines and Natanis Pond.

The re-enactment was a fitting memorial to the 1100 brave soldiers and officers who followed General Arnold through the wilderness of northern Maine, through snow, flood and ice, famine and disease in response to George Washington's directive of early September:

To launch an expedition with all speed to capture Quebec City, the stronghold of the British forces.

Bateau demonstration
on the Kennebec River
at Old Point in Madison.

He MUST have lied about his age!

Bateau crew at ease — Cathedral Pines on
the south bank of Dead River in Eustis.

The Arnold Expedition Parade in Stratton, Maine.

Members of the Expedition portraying an Indian princess, a French Jesuit priest and others.

Old Point on the Kennebec River in Madison. This was the site of the old Norridgewock Indian Village, destroyed by the English in 1724, and the Father Rasle monument is located there. To the Indians it was a sacred vale and the most beautiful place they could imagine.

Whittier was so touched by the tragic massacre there that he wrote the beautiful poem "Mog Megone," of which a few excerpts follow:

'Tis morning over Norridgewock,
On tree and wigwam, wave and rock.
Bathed in the autumnal sunshine, stirred
At intervals by breeze and bird,
And wearing all the hues which glow
In heaven's own pure and perfect bow,
That glorious picture of the air,
Which summer's light-robed angel forms

On the dark ground of fading storms,
With pencil dipped in sunbeams there,
And, stretching out, on either hand,
O'er all that wide and unshorn land,
Till weary of its gorgeousness,
The aching and the dazzled eye
Rests, gladdened, on the calm blue sky,
Slumbers the mighty wilderness!

Breaking a log jam — Skowhegan.

The last log drive in the United States took place on the Kennebec in 1976. No more will we see brawny river drivers walk on the logs — "ride the sticks" — or break a log jam with infinite patience and skill. No more will we see a bateau man maneuver a raft of logs to the top of a sluice at Wyman Dam. The last Kennebec bateau has been sent to the Smithsonian Institution and the steamer *Katahdin* will become a museum in Greenville.

Photo by C. Lancaster

Madison Paper Mill in the early 1950's with a 30,000 cord pile of logs in the yard.

Greenville, situated at the foot of
Moosehead Lake, is the gateway to the
northern Maine wilderness and the
Allagash country. It boasts beautiful
scenery, historic lumber barons' homes,
and the Squaw Mountain all seasons
resort. It was one of the first villages to
attract tourists, including Thoreau and
Lowell who visited there about 1850.
Both wrote about the region, Thoreau in
The Maine Woods and Lowell in *A
Moosehead Journal.*

Moose River Marina in Rockwood, near
the mouth of Moosehead Lake's most
important inlet.

Settlers and lumbermen were attracted to our northern Maine wilderness by the magnificent forests of pine and spruce. When white pine became scarce, the spruce became the sought after tree. One of our Maine writers, Holman Day, called the spruce tree "King of the forest" in his book *King Spruce*.

One may still see magnificent white pine trees in Cathedral Pines in Eustis. This fine specimen was photographed there.

The waters of Moxie Pond flow into the Kennebec River about four miles north of the Forks, via Moxie Stream.

Wyman Dam, stretching between the townships of Moscow and Pleasant Ridge, was built in 1930. It is an imposing structure, 3,000 feet across the top and 150 feet above the crest of the water on the downstream side. It changed the face of the river and its valley from Caratunk down to Bingham.

A towboat hauling a boom of logs several acres in extent down Wyman Lake toward Wyman Dam.

When Wyman Dam was finished, the
waters of the Kennebec backed up
almost to the village of Caratunk,
forming a magnificent body of water 12
miles long. Former hills became islands,
mouths of streams and valleys became
coves, and the road was moved halfway
up the side of Mount Baker and other
hills to provide one of the most scenic
drives in Maine, especially in October.

Autumn on Wyman Lake.

Bingham was named for William Bingham, the richest and one of the most influential men during the American Revolution, who purchased one million acres of surrounding land shortly after the war.

It is the gateway to the huge lumbering and hunting areas in northern Somerset County including the Dead River watershed and the beautiful Wyman Lake region.

It is situated on a beautiful stretch of the Kennebec River. This picture was taken entering from the south on Route 201.

The Forks, where the Kennebec and Dead Rivers meet. Route 201 crosses the Kennebec River here.

Thrills and chills greet the adventurous on the upper Kennebec and Penobscot whitewater rafting trips.

The Kennebec Gorge as seen from the boat landing at the foot of Harris Dam at the outlet of Indian Pond.

Maine
captured
in color

villages & their buildings...

St. Philip's Episcopal Church, Wiscasset

Steeple of Union Meeting House, Farmington Falls.
The Tower, Belfry and Spire
of this church are after the style of Wren.
The building is on the National Register.

Steeples in the Sky, Congregational Church, New Sharon.

Interior South
Solon Meeting
House

"Little Brown
Church" Round
Pond Village

A quiet day at Back Cove.

A view on the Damariscotta River at East Boothbay.

Readin, Writin and Rithmetic!

This one room, country schoolhouse, long unused, was discovered on Route 215 near Damariscotta Mills.
The road formerly known as "The Pond Road" offers fine views of rolling farm lands and the lovely Damariscotta Lake.

Trudi's flower garden

Sheepscot River

Lilac Time

Lilacs adorn the gray clapboarded sides of the oldest house
in Wiscasset built in 1763.
It may be found overlooking the Sheepscot River.

Two beautiful and historic buildings on the Common in
Wiscasset. The Lincoln County Courthouse, built in 1824,
is still in use. The First Congregational Church, also still in
use, dates from 1763.

A Typical Maine Home and reflection — Bristol

The Jewett homestead, locally called "The Parsonage" was built in 1760 by one of the early settlers of Head Tide, it remains a beautiful example of our 18th century Maine architecture.

This Is My Country
by Robert P. Tristram Coffin

This is my country, bitter as the sea,
Pungent with the fir and bayberry.
An island meadow, stonewalled, high
    and lost,
With August cranberries touched red
    by frost.
Two hours of sun before the fog erases
The walls on walls of trees trimmed
    sharp as laces.
A house behind the last hill of them all,
And after that, the lonesome seagulls'
    call;
A juniper on a windy ledge,
Splendor of granite on the world's bright
    edge,
A heron on the beach and one on wing,
Wind wrapped round each last and
    living thing,
A lighthouse like a diamond, cut and
    sharp,
And all the trees like strings upon
    a harp.

Round Pond Reflections

Windsor Group entertaining with dances of the past — Yankee Peddler's Day at Pownalborough Courthouse, Dresden.

Montpelier, the restored General Knox
Mansion, Thomaston.

When General Knox Kept Open House
By Holman F. Day
"Kin O' Katahdin"

From Penobscot to the Kennebec, from
    Moosehead to the sea,
Was spread the forest barony of Knox, bluff
    Knox;
And the Great house on the Georges it
    open was and free,
And around it, all uncounted, roved its
    bonny herds and flocks.

Its beds were an hundred, they were
    tumbled every day
By the guests and by the pensioners
    of Knox, good Knox.
They were joyous in their coming and were
    loath to go away,
For the welcome was unstinted and the
    larder had no locks.

Damariscotta, a lovely town with many beautiful old homes, fan-lighted doorways, and historic churches, is situated at the head of the Damariscotta River and is the gateway to the Pemaquid peninsula.

Williams Dam at Solon was built on the site of Caratunk Falls, famous as far back as Indian days when the Abenakis called it "Devil's Falls." Arnold also had reason to call it that, as the velocity of the rushing water compressed between two high cliffs made it a very difficult spot for his army to carry around.

As one drives down a long hill coming from Blue Hill, the pretty village of Orland appears spread out at the foot like an old fashioned picture postcard.

Skowhegan is the county seat of Somerset County, situated on one of the few bends in the Kennebec River. Its Abenaki Indian name means "a place where they watched to spear salmon as they passed up over the falls."

Country road between Skowhegan and Waterville

Skowhegan's pretty streets and views of the river make it a very attractive town. Its history is interesting. The first two settlers to spend a winter there were two young boys: Eli Weston, age 11, and 16-year-old Isaac Smith. It has gained fame in later years as the birthplace and residence of Margaret Chase Smith, Maine's beloved former Senator.

Maine
captured in color

the woodland trail . . .

The Forest Floor

What fun to walk along a woodland trail, shedding the cares of a
busy day, and searching for the secrets of the forest floor.

Look carefully and step lightly lest some of nature's masterpieces
be overlooked and crushed as many are tiny and hidden from all
but the most perceptive eye.

The searcher must often drop to his knees, perhaps in a woodland
puddle, to get close enough to appreciate the small plants and
fungi which crowd our woods.

Pink Lady's Slipper

We find a charming description of this native orchid
in an old 1893 flower book.

Graceful and tall the slender drooping stem
With two broad leaves below,
Shapely the flower so lightly poised between,
and warm her rosy glow.

Elaine Goodale

The Rhodora

Rhodora! if the sages ask thee why
This charm is wasted on earth and sky,
Tell them, dear, that if eyes were made for seeing,
Then beauty is its own excuse for being;
Why thou wert there, O rival of the rose!
I never thought to ask, I never knew;
But, in my simple ignorance, suppose
The self-same Power that brought me there brought you.

Ralph Waldo Emerson

Match Stick Lichen or British Soldiers
Among the smallest of the woods miniatures these handsome lichens nestled in a bed of moss are only about a quarter of an inch tall and really look like the head of an old fashioned match.

Purple Lilacs remindful of Grandma's garden
where around Memorial Day their sweet scent filled the air —
I remember picking armfuls —
One bouquet to be placed before the Civil War soldier on his granite shaft in front of the library —
The others deposited with great solemnity in the cemetery.

Blue Violets and Bluets

Looking for combination bouquets can be an exciting quest for the flower lover. Nature proves to be a master at flower arranging, mixing colors and forms with gay abandon. This lovely grouping was found in front of a house in Day's Ferry where the lady of the house told me that violets and bluets were taking over her lawn. Well, this can happen when the environment is right but what a pretty carpet they do make.

Wild Rose

What's in a Name?
That which we call a Rose
By any other name would smell as sweet.

Shakespeare

Winds of the Wilderness

Winds of the wilderness, sing me again
The songs of my childhood, from woodland and glen:
The soft lullabies of a musical brook
That sang me to sleep in a shadowed nook;
The distant call of a whip-poor-will,
And a lone star shining o'er yonder hill;
And the old brown goose, in the evening cool,
Winging her way to some deep pool;
The mystic mountains so far from me . . .
These are the things my eyes would see.

Winds of the wilderness, blow soft, blow light
Across that mirrored lake tonight
Sailing again in my old canoe
Down a sparkling path of golden hue;
Rippling waves that softly break
On a crescent shore where brown deer wait;
Drifting along through starshine and moon,
And the far-off cry of a lonely loon;
Knowing the woods make a circle dim
Where the voices of night are notes in a hymn.

By Elizabeth Hamilton Hartsgrove

Carrying Place Stream, the outlet of East Carry Pond, which
empties into the Kennebec River near Caratunk.

Let in through all the trees
Come the strange rays; the forest depths
    are bright;
Their sunny colored foliage, in the breeze,
    Twinkles, like beams of light.

                    William Cullen Bryant

Road scenes — Baxter State Park

Two autumn views on the Carrabassett

The long bright days of summer swiftly
    passed,
The dry leaves whirled in autumn's
    rising blast,
And evening cloud and whitening
    sunrise rime
Told of the coming of the winter-time.

John Greenleaf Whittier

Double Top Mountain in Baxter State Park changes its appearance with every change of the weather and season. It overlooks the Nesowadnehunk River as it winds its way to the West Branch of the Penobscot River.

Sugarloaf Mountain has become famous as a skiing resort during the last few years. It is situated in beautiful countryside with the Carrabassett River flowing along its base. In fact the river's source is on the northern slope of the mountain. The Carrabassett valley is now a far cry from the old days when it was a tiny woodland settlement with a narrow gauge railroad passing through on its way to the terminus at Bigelow Station.

Mount Katahdin, Maine's highest peak
and favorite of Maine climbers, is also
the start of the two thousand mile long
Appalachian Trail.

Kidney Pond, Baxter State Park

Cooking out at Roaring Brook Campground
on Katahdin Stream

Big Niagara on the Nesowadnehunk River
in Baxter State Park

On the Banks of the Carrabassett, near Kingfield

For he shall be as a tree planted by the waters, and that spreadeth out her roots by the river, and shall not see when heat cometh, but her leaf shall be green. . . . .

Jeremiah 17:8

The Wire Bridge spans the Carrabassett River in the Village of New Portland. The parts for this bridge were brought from England by sailing ship in the early part of the 1800's. From the wharf in Augusta they were transported overland by Ox-Team. It has stood the ravages of time and Spring Freshets well and is still in use.

The Carrabassett is a delightful tributary of the Kennebec, wending its way from Sugarloaf Mountain through Kingfield, under the historic Wire Bridge at New Portland, and between fields and farmlands. It is a favorite of white water canoeists.

The Abenaki Indians who lived in northern Somerset County called waterways such as this "Rivers Shod with Rocks."

Autumn on the Carrabassett — This stream becomes ravishingly beautiful when its thick border of birches and maples takes on its Fall dress. To enjoy the sight follow this tributary of the Kennebec from North Anson to the Canadian border and then turn around and enjoy it a second time on the way back.

Falls on Katahdin Stream, Baxter State Park

It is hard to imagine a lovelier picnic spot than Cathedral Pines on Route 27 in the township of Eustis. The huge grove of white pines will provide background music for your meal as there is a constant whispering of pine needles and boughs set off by even the gentlest breeze. Dead River flows at the foot of the cliff and Mount Bigelow overlooks the whole scene. A nearby road ascends to the summit of Eustis Ridge, from which a spectacular view of Mount Bigelow, Flagstaff Lake and the surrounding countryside may be seen.

The deer, half seen are to covert wending. . . .

Sir Walter Scott

The majestic Moose frequents the lake country of northern Maine.
They especially like the shallow water where they can wade, lumbering along slowly.
This one rounded a point of land at Kidney Pond Camp and approached the lodge to cause the complete disruption of the dinner hour as everyone ran for cameras.

Arriving at Enchanted Pond

Enchanted Pond is the site of extensive lumbering operations of the late 1800's. The camps are now long deserted and overgrown.

View of Shutdown Mountain from Bulldog Camp Boat Landing — Enchanted Pond.

The inlet of Enchanted Pond, and the start of the trail up Enchanted Stream to the upper pond.

Only the rustling of pine trees and the gurgle of Enchanted Stream at the outlet breaks the silence of the wilderness of Upper Enchanted Pond. The occasional intruder speaks and walks softly to guard the peaceful atmosphere.

Lone Camp on Enchanted Pond

Canoe Landing — Upper Enchanted Pond

A log cabin at Bulldog Camp on Enchanted Pond, one of Maine's famous lumbering areas at the turn of the century.
To lumbermen it was simply "The Enchanted."

This mountain brook provides the cabins at Bulldog Camp with running water — cold not hot!

Trout for breakfast

Remnants of the famous mile and a quarter long H K McKinney Log Sluice on Enchanted Stream circa 1883.

A Pheasant, Enchanted Pond

Maine
captured
in color

life on the shore . . .

Boothbay Shores

The Sterling Pierce Cottage on Wyman Lake

Before Wyman Dam was built, Mr. Pierce was told that his Kennebec River bank farm would be submerged
when the new Wyman Lake was formed. He consulted Central Maine Power Company plans
and proceeded to build a cottage in the deep woods on a hill, to the amusement of his friends.
Now Mr. Pierce's son and family sit on their front porch enjoying the view down the length of beautiful Wyman Lake.

Island Living (Yankee Coast)

There is a psychology, and there is a poetry, to living on an island.
A good deal of Maine living is island living, the coast being what it is.
When you splinter up a diamond on the edge of the sea, there are bound to be many chips scattered about on the water.
The brightest people, from the first explorers on, took to the islands first as the likeliest places to keep alive and happy on.
Water was fences and walls and moats and stockades, from time immemorial, as well as the best roads.
So people settled on the islands. . . .

Robert P. Tristram Coffin

Nubble Light, York

Rachel Carson's tide pool. Much of the research for *The Sea Around Us* was done at this lovely pool in New Harbor.

A Tide Pool Mirror, reflecting Pemaquid Light

This fishing shack on Bailey Island brightens up the shore with its red door and colorful floats.

"Sarah Orne Jewett Country"
Excerpts from *The Country of the Pointed Firs* by Sarah Orne Jewett

The tide was in, and the wide harbor
was surrounded by its dark woods,
and the small wooden houses stood
as near as they could get to the landing.
Mrs. Todd's was the last house on the way inland.
The gray ledges of the rocky shore
were well covered with sod in most places,
and the pasture bayberry and wild roses
grew thick among them.

We were standing where there was a fine view of the harbor
and its long stretches of shore all covered by the great army
of pointed firs, darkly cloaked
and standing as if they wished to embark.
As we looked far seaward among the outer islands,
the trees seemed to march seaward still,
going steadily over the heights and down to the water's edge.

On the lonely coast of Maine stood a small gray house facing the morning light. All the weatherbeaten houses of that region face the sea apprehensively, like the women who live in them.

. . . . The few houses made the most of their seaward view, and there was a gaiety and determined floweriness in their bits of garden ground.

The small-paned high windows in the peaks of their steep gables were like knowing eyes that watched the harbor and the far sealine beyond, or looked northward all along the shore and its background of spruces and balsam firs.

When one really knows a village like this and its surroundings, it is like becoming acquainted with a single person. The process of falling in love at first sight is as final as it is swift in such a case, but the growth of true friendship may be a lifelong affair.

It had been growing gray and cloudy, like the first evening of autumn, and a shadow had fallen on the darkening shore. Suddenly we looked and a gleam of golden sunshine struck the outer islands, and one of them shone out clear in the light, and revealed itself in a compelling way to our eyes.

Mrs. Todd was looking off across the bay with a face full of affection and interest. . . .
The sunburst on that outer island made it seem like a sudden revelation of the world beyond this which some believe to be so near.

Before us lay a splendid world of sea and shore. The autumn colors already brightened the landscape; and here and there at the edge of a dark tract of pointed firs stood a row of bright swamp maples like scarlet flowers. The blue sea and the great tide inlets were untroubled by the lightest winds.

Pemaquid Lighthouse

How many ships have I warned in winter gales?
How many souls have I saved
With my strong and steady beacon?

Trawler at Home Port at Close of Day

Returning Osprey with a Gift for the Nest

Learning Nature's Ways, Ocean Point

Three Captains Chairs, on the dock at South Bristol
After the fishing fleet is in and the gear stored, the captains settle down here for a round of tall tales.

The wide variety of Maine's long crooked coast line is a delight.
We can see bold headlands at Monhegan and Mount Desert Island and gently graded beaches at Old Orchard, Wells and Reid State Park. The endless parade of breaking, foam-capped waves lulls us with their beauty and 'tis said that every seventh one is a Grand-Daddy!

Boothbay harbor looking toward the east side of the harbor

East Boothbay as seen from the Mill Pond

"Glad Tidings" is its real name, but our grandchildren call it "The Pirate Ship."

The smell of the sea still lingers around this Port Clyde Fishing Shack!

The view from my window — Montgomery Point on the Damariscotta River. Black marker buoy number 7.

Maine's coastal villages have a charm all their own.

Stonington draws us to her ragged shore
with its boats left high and dry by the outgoing tide
and the fishing shacks gaily bedecked with rows
of multi-colored floats.

Wharf at Pratts Island Bridge, Southport

Camden Harbor, home port for a large fleet of handsome windjammers.

Crowds gather in Friendship to watch the annual Friendship Sloop races.

The Rockbound Coast, Acadia National Park

Monhegan Shore

A Breaking Wave, Ocean Point

The water crashed down with overwhelming flood,
Dashes over the natural crags in beautiful confusion. . . .

Whittier

Full many a gem of purist ray
    serene
The dark unfathomed caves
    of ocean bear
            Thomas Gray

Left by the Tide, a tide pool at Ocean Point

Dock Still Life, Weatherbeaten Lobster Floats at South Bristol

Launching Day, John G. Alden Boatyard, East Boothbay

Fishing shack reflections near Tenants Harbor

Bass Island Lighthouse

House in Blue Hill

Steeple — Congregational Church, Ellsworth

Windjammer Days

But come. With tools of bronze you must hew tall timbers
And build yourself a boat, sufficiently broad-beamed
And high-decked to carry you over the misty deep sea.
I will stock it with bread and water and warming red wine . . . .
And give it a tail wind
Too, that completely unharmed you may reach your own country.

Homer's *Odyssey*

Victory Chimes, approaching Boothbay Harbor

Little Christmas Cove, Southport

My friend said, "How would you like to see ten dories all swinging at anchor in a pretty cove?"
We hurried there and just as she had said, there they were —
lazily floating in a long line, up and down as the tide ebbed and flowed.

Relics of the Past

These two hulks, rotting away just south of the bridge over the Sheepscot River
in Wiscasset draw tourists with cameras by the hundreds. Both ships were built in time
to cash in on the First World War sailing boom.

The *Hesper* (the one lacking masts) was built in 1918 in Massachusetts,
after which the 210-foot long, 4-masted schooner made trips to Portugal and Venezuela
in the coal and lumber trade. Plagued by several accidents and a grounding,
she was laid up in Rockland, Maine, and finally landed in Wiscasset
on September 1, 1932, where she has lain ever since.

The *Luther Little*, 204 feet long, was built in 1917 and made her last sail
while still in good condition. Retired in the middle 1920s, due to lack of cargoes and
shortage of crews, she was brought to Wiscasset in 1932 to settle down in the mud
of the Sheepscot River beside the *Hesper*.

Laura B leaving Monhegan

Port Clyde

Stonington

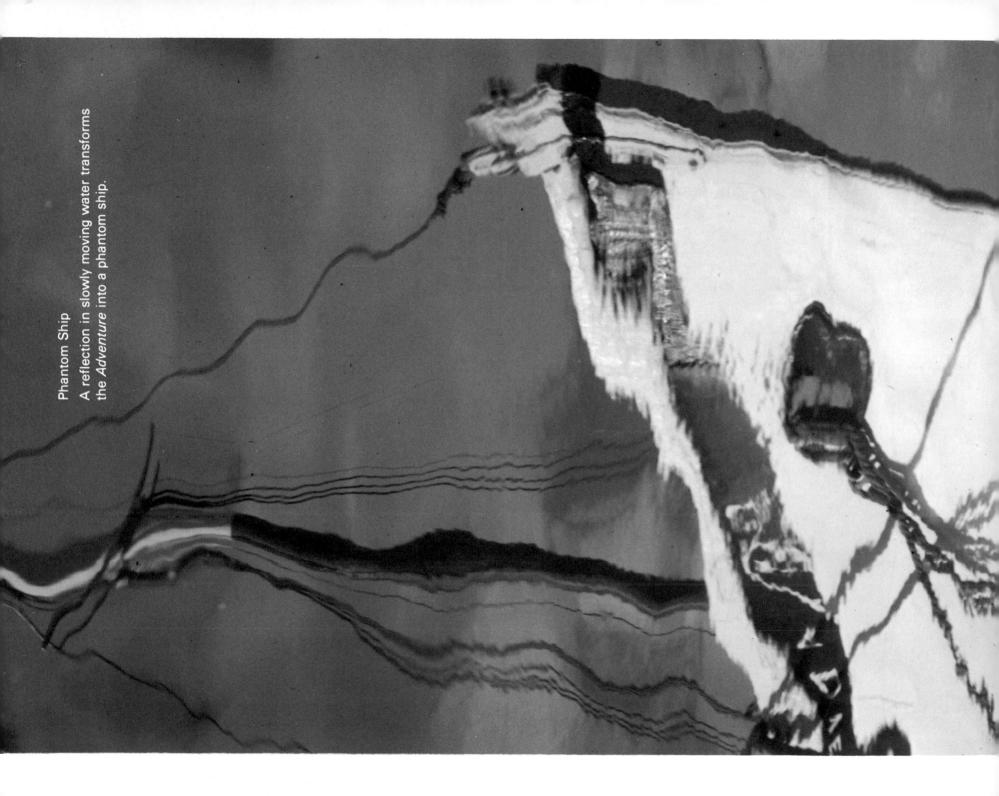

Phantom Ship

A reflection in slowly moving water transforms the *Adventure* into a phantom ship.

Friendship Sloop Days

Annual races and get-together
of Friendship sloops in Friendship

Waiting for the Race to Start

Townsend Gut, near Boothbay Harbor

Windjammer Days

Dragger *Star* in fog bound harbor

A Sunset at Seal Point Cottage

by Frances L. Mace

From the gray rocks that walled the beach
  We watched the sinking sun,
Till as the last cloud curtain rolled
Across his drooping crown of gold,
  We said "The day is done."

The gateway of the West was closed,
  The King was seen no more;
And in the pensive even-glow
We strayed with tranquil step and slow
  Along the grassy shore.

But as we gazed, the Eastern sky
  Was lighted up anew:
Long bars of gleaming, crystal green
Across the heavens a dazzling sheen
  Of sudden splendor threw.

The waves along the wide-stretched bay
  Awoke as if from sleep,
And trembling in a strange delight,
Repelled the coming gloom of night
  And drank the radiance deep.

Then purple banners richly wrought
  With many a golden sign,
Waved glorious o'er the heavenly plain,
And all the billows shone again
  With blazonry divine.

And ever as a brighter hue
  Illumed the sky and flood,
The mountains on the further shore,
A darker, dreamier aspect wore,
  And with us watching stood.

Still flushed the deepening tints, and now
  A lurid lustre came,
And as with sacrificial fire
The orient burned with splendors dire,
  The sea with tossing flame!

And once again a wondrous change —
  For over all the skies
Swift fading as the night came down,
Were leagues of roses, brightly blown,
  Of pure, celestial dyes!

Fast as they bloomed in heaven they shed
  Their petals on the sea!
Till in a rosy wave of light
They vanished from our raptured sight,
  A twilight mystery.

Homeward beneath the whispering trees
  We walked and spoke no word;
For we had seen with living eyes,
On sunset sea and sunset skies,
  The glory of the Lord.

(Verses from very old book circa 1880)

Afterglow